W9-BPQ-095

The Significance of the Frontier in American History

Frederick J. Turner

The Significance of the Frontier
in American History

ANNUAL REPORT

OF THE

AMERICAN HISTORICAL ASSOCIATION

FOR

THE YEAR 1893.

WASHINGTON:
GOVERNMENT PRINTING OFFICE.
1894.

FIFTY-THIRD CONGRESS, SECOND SESSION.

MARCH 5, 1894.—In the Senate of the United States. The Vice-President presented the following Annual Report of the American Historical Association. Referred to the Committee on Printing and ordered to be printed.

II

LETTER OF SUBMITTAL.

SMITHSONIAN INSTITUTION,
Washington, D. C., March 3, 1894.

To the Congress of the United States:

In accordance with the act of incorporation of the American Historical Association, approved January 4, 1889, I have the honor to submit to Congress the annual report of said association for the year 1893.

I have the honor to be, very respectfully, your obedient servant,

S. P. LANGLEY,
Secretary of the Smithsonian Institution.

Hon. ADLAI E. STEVENSON,
President of the Senate.

Hon. CHARLES F. CRISP,
Speaker of the House.

III

ACT OF INCORPORATION.

Be it enacted by the Senate and House of Representatives of the United States of America in Congress assembled, That Andrew D. White, of Ithaca, in the State of New York; George Bancroft, of Washington, in the District of Columbia; Justin Winsor, of Cambridge, in the State of Massachusetts; William F. Poole, of Chicago, in the State of Illinois; Herbert B. Adams, of Baltimore, in the State of Maryland; Clarence W. Bowen, of Brooklyn, in the State of New York; their associates and successors, are hereby created in the District of Columbia a body corporate and politic, by the name of the American Historical Association, for. the promotion of historical studies, the collection and preservation of historical manuscripts, and for kindred purposes in the interest of American history and of history in America. Said association is authorized to hold real and personal estate in the District of Columbia, so far only as may be necessary to its lawful ends, to an amount not exceeding five hundred thousand dollars, to adopt a constitution, and to make by-laws not inconsistent with law. Said association shall have its principal office at Washington, in the District of Columbia, and may hold its annual meetings in such places as the said incorporators shall determine. Said association shall report annually to the Secretary of the Smithsonian Institution concerning its proceedings and the condition of historical study in America. Said Secretary shall communicate to Congress the whole of such reports, or such portions thereof as he shall see fit. The regents of the Smithsonian Institution are authorized to permit said association to deposit its collections, manuscripts, books, pamphlets, and other material for history in the Smithsonian Institution or in the National Museum, at their discretion, upon such conditions and under such rules as they shall prescribe.

[Approved, January 4, 1889.]

IV

LETTER OF TRANSMITTAL.

AMERICAN HISTORICAL ASSOCIATION,
Baltimore, Md., February 24, 1894.

SIR: In compliance with the act of incorporation of the American Historical Association, approved January 4, 1889, which requires that "said association shall report annually to the Secretary of the Smithsonian Institution concerning its proceedings and the condition of historical study in America," I have the honor to transmit herewith my general report of the proceedings of the American Historical Association at their ninth annual meeting, held in Chicago, July 11–13, 1893. In addition to the general summary of proceedings, I send also the inaugural address of Dr. James B. Angell, president of the the association, and some of the papers read at the Chicago meeting. In order to show the condition and progress of historical study in America, I append to the report of the association certain contributions toward a bibliography of American history, from 1888 to 1892, adapted from reports to the Jahresbericht der Geschichtswissenschaft of Berlin, by Dr. John Martin Vincent.

Very respectfully,

HERBERT B. ADAMS,
Secretary.

Prof. S. P. LANGLEY,
Secretary of the Smithsonian Institution.

AMERICAN HISTORICAL ASSOCIATION.

Organized at Saratoga, N. Y., September 10, 1884.

OFFICERS FOR 1894.

President :
HENRY ADAMS,
Washington, D. C.

Vice-Presidents :
EDWARD G. MASON,
Chicago, Ill.
HON. GEORGE F. HOAR,
Worcester, Mass.

Treasurer :
CLARENCE WINTHROP BOWEN, PH. D.,
Fulton and Nassau Streets, New York City.

Secretary :
HERBERT B. ADAMS, PH. D., LL. D.,
Professor of History in the Johns Hopkins University, Baltimore, Md.

Assistant Secretary and Curator :
A. HOWARD CLARK,
Curator of Historical Collections, National Museum, Washington, D. C.

Executive Council :
(In addition to the above-named officers.)
HON. ANDREW D. WHITE, LL. D., L. H. D.,
Ithaca, N. Y.
JUSTIN WINSOR, LL. D.,
Cambridge, Mass.
CHARLES KENDALL ADAMS, LL. D.,
President of University of Wisconsin, Madison.
HON. WILLIAM WIRT HENRY,
Richmond, Va.
WILLIAM F. POOLE, LL. D.,
Librarian of Newberry Library, Chicago.
HON. JOHN JAY, LL. D.,
New York City.
JAMES B. ANGELL, LL. D.,
President of University of Michigan, Ann Arbor.
G. BROWN GOODE, PH. D., LL. D.,
Assistant Secretary Smithsonian Institution, in Charge of the National Museum.
JOHN GEORGE BOURINOT, C. M. G., LL. D., D. C. L.,
Clerk of the Canadian House of Commons.
J. B. McMASTER,
Professor of History in the University of Pennsylvania, Philadelphia.
GEORGE B. ADAMS,
Professor of History in Yale University, New Haven.

XVIII.—THE SIGNIFICANCE OF THE FRONTIER IN AMERICAN HISTORY.

By PROFESSOR FREDERICK J. TURNER,

OF THE UNIVERSITY OF WISCONSIN.

Foreword

Frederick Jackson Turner's "The Significance of the Frontier in American History," first read as a paper at the meeting of the American Historical Association, held at the Chicago World's Fair on July 12, 1893, changed the course of interpretation of American history for a generation and has profoundly influenced the explanation of the growth of American civilization. Turner's essay was first printed in 1894 in the *Proceedings of the State Historical Society of Wisconsin... 1893* and reprinted in the *Annual Report of the American Historical Association for the Year 1893* (1894), a facsimile of which is reproduced here.

Turner himself grew up in a region full of memories of frontier conditions, for he was born in 1861 at Portage, Wisconsin, where explorers, trappers, traders, and frontiersmen for many years had passed, on their way West. He was educated at the University of Wisconsin, taking an A.B. degree in 1884 and an M.A. in 1888. For the doctorate at the Johns Hopkins University in 1890 he presented a dissertation on "The Character and Influence of the Indian Trade in Wisconsin." By 1889 he was an assistant professor at the University of Wisconsin; he became a full professor in 1891. Turner remained at Wisconsin until 1910, when he was called to Harvard, where he stayed until his retirement in 1924. He spent his last years at the Huntington Library in California. He died on March 14, 1932.

Turner's seminal essay on the frontier was prompted by a statement in the Census Report of 1890 asserting that the "frontier of settlement" no longer existed and it would have no further "place in the census reports." To Turner this declaration had enormous importance. "This brief official statement marks the closing of a great historic movement," he pointed out. "Up to our day American history has been in a large degree the history of the colonization of the Great West. The existence of an area of free land, its continuous recession, and the advance of American settlement westward, explain American development." This thesis he developed in his paper. As he saw it, the growth of American civilization "has exhibited not merely advance along a single line, but a return to primitive conditions on a continually advancing frontier line, and a new development in that area. American social development has been continually beginning over again on the frontier. This perennial rebirth, this fluidity of American life, this expansion westward with its new opportunities, its continuous touch with the simplicity of primitive society, furnish the forces dominating American character."

Turner maintained that the unique experience of Americans in moving into a frontier zone of free land helped to explain their independence of spirit, their zeal for democratic institutions, their elimination of non-essentials in government, their nationalism, and most of the qualities that went into the "American character." Turner himself set forth his views modestly and tentatively. Some of his disciples became more dogmatic. Around him and his ideas, a whole school of history developed. In recent years, fresh appraisals of the growth of American society have tended to modify the Turner thesis and in some instances to refute it.

A brief account of Turner will be found in the *Dictionary of American Biography*. One of the best analyses of Turner's views is that by Carl Becker in *American Masters of Social Science*, edited by H. W. Odum (New York, 1927). A useful essay critical of the Turner hypothesis is that by Benjamin F. Wright, Jr., "American Democracy and the Frontier," *Yale Review* (winter issue, 1931).

The Significance
of the Frontier
in American History

by Frederick J. Turner

READEX MICROPRINT

THE SIGNIFICANCE OF THE FRONTIER IN AMERICAN HISTORY.*

By FREDERICK J. TURNER.

In a recent bulletin of the Superintendent of the Census for 1890 appear these significant words: "Up to and including 1880 the country had a frontier of settlement, but at present the unsettled area has been so broken into by isolated bodies of settlement that there can hardly be said to be a frontier line. In the discussion of its extent, its westward movement, etc., it can not, therefore, any longer have a place in the census reports." This brief official statement marks the closing of a great historic movement. Up to our own day American history has been in a large degree the history of the colonization of the Great West. The existence of an area of free land, its continuous recession, and the advance of American settlement westward, explain American development.

Behind institutions, behind constitutional forms and modifications, lie the vital forces that call these organs into life and shape them to meet changing conditions. The peculiarity of American institutions is, the fact that they have been compelled to adapt themselves to the changes of an expanding people—to the changes involved in crossing a continent, in winning a wilderness, and in developing at each area of this progress out of the primitive economic and political conditions of the frontier into the complexity of city life. Said Calhoun in 1817, "We are great, and rapidly—I was about to say fearfully—growing!"† So saying, he touched the distinguishing feature of American life. All peoples show development; the germ theory of politics has been sufficiently emphasized. In the case of most nations, however, the development

---

* Since the meeting of the American Historical Association, this paper has also been given as an address to the State Historical Society of Wisconsin, December 14, 1893. I have to thank the Secretary of the Society, Mr. Reuben G. Thwaites, for securing valuable material for my use in the preparation of the paper.
† Abridgment of Debates of Congress, v., p. 706.

has occurred in a limited area; and if the nation has expanded, it has met other growing peoples whom it has conquered. But in the case of the United States we have a different phenomenon. Limiting our attention to the Atlantic coast, we have the familiar phenomenon of the evolution of institutions in a limited area, such as the rise of representative government; the differentiation of simple colonial governments into complex organs; the progress from primitive industrial society, without division of labor, up to manufacturing civilization. But we have in addition to this a recurrence of the process of evolution in each western area reached in the process of expansion. Thus American development has exhibited not merely advance along a single line, but a return to primitive conditions on a continually advancing frontier line, and a new development for that area. American social development has been continually beginning over again on the frontier. This perennial rebirth, this fluidity of American life, this expansion westward with its new opportunities, its continuous touch with the simplicity of primitive society, furnish the forces dominating American character. The true point of view in the history of this nation is not the Atlantic coast, it is the great West. Even the slavery struggle, which is made so exclusive an object of attention by writers like Prof. von Holst, occupies its important place in American history because of its relation to westward expansion.

In this advance, the frontier is the outer edge of the wave—the meeting point between savagery and civilization. Much has been written about the frontier from the point of view of border warfare and the chase, but as a field for the serious study of the economist and the historian it has been neglected.

The American frontier is sharply distinguished from the European frontier—a fortified boundary line running through dense populations. The most significant thing about the American frontier is, that it lies at the hither edge of free land. In the census reports it is treated as the margin of that settlement which has a density of two or more to the square mile. The term is an elastic one, and for our purposes does not need sharp definition. We shall consider the whole frontier belt, including the Indian country and the outer margin of the "settled area" of the census reports. This paper will make no attempt to treat the subject exhaustively; its aim is simply to call attention to the frontier as a fertile field for investigation, and to suggest some of the problems which arise in connection with it.

In the settlement of America we have to observe how European life entered the continent, and how America modified and developed that life and reacted on Europe. Our early history is the study of European germs developing in an American environment. Too exclusive attention has been paid by institutional students to the Germanic origins, too little to the American factors. The frontier is the line of most rapid and effective Americanization. The wilderness masters the colonist. It finds him a European in dress, industries, tools, modes of travel, and thought. It takes him from the railroad car and puts him in the birch canoe. It strips off the garments of civilization and arrays him in the hunting shirt and the moccasin. It puts him in the log cabin of the Cherokee and Iroquois and runs an Indian palisade around him. Before long he has gone to planting Indian corn and plowing with a sharp stick; he shouts the war cry and takes the scalp in orthodox Indian fashion. In short, at the frontier the environment is at first too strong for the man. He must accept the conditions which it furnishes, or perish, and so he fits himself into the Indian clearings and follows the Indian trails. Little by little he transforms the wilderness, but the outcome is not the old Europe, not simply the development of Germanic germs, any more than the first phenomenon was a case of reversion to the Germanic mark. The fact is, that here is a new product that is American. At first, the frontier was the Atlantic coast. It was the frontier of Europe in a very real sense. Moving westward, the frontier became more and more American. As successive terminal moraines result from successive glaciations, so each frontier leaves its traces behind it, and when it becomes a settled area the region still partakes of the frontier characteristics. Thus the advance of the frontier has meant a steady movement away from the influence of Europe, a steady growth of independence on American lines. And to study this advance, the men who grew up under these conditions, and the political, economic, and social results of it, is to study the really American part of our history.

STAGES OF FRONTIER ADVANCE.

In the course of the seventeenth century the frontier was advanced up the Atlantic river courses, just beyond the "fall line," and the tidewater region became the settled area. In the first half of the eighteenth century another advance occurred. Traders followed the Delaware and Shawnese Indians to the Ohio as early as the end of the first quarter of the century.* Gov. Spotswood, of Virginia, made an expedition in 1714 across the Blue Ridge. The end of the first quarter of the century saw the advance of the Scotch-Irish and the Palatine Germans up the Shenandoah Valley into the western part of Virginia, and along the Piedmont region of the Carolinas.† The Germans in New York pushed the frontier of settlement up the Mohawk to German Flats.‡ In Pennsylvania the town of Bedford indicates the line of settlement. Settlements had begun on New River, a branch of the Kanawha, and on the sources of the Yadkin and French Broad.§ The King attempted to arrest the advance by his proclamation of 1763,‖ forbidding settlements beyond the sources of the rivers flowing into the Atlantic; but in vain. In the period of the Revolution the frontier crossed the Alleghanies into Kentucky and Tenneseee, and the upper waters of the Ohio were settled.¶ When the first census was taken in 1790, the continuous settled area was bounded by a line which ran near the coast of Maine, and included New England except a portion of Vermont and New Hampshire, New York along the Hudson and up the Mohawk about Schenectady, eastern and southern Pennsylvania, Virginia well across the Shenandoah Valley,

---

* Bancroft (1860 ed.), III, pp. 344, 345, citing Logan MSS.; [Mitchell] Contest in America, etc. (1752), p. 237.

† Kercheval, History of the Valley; Bernheim, German Settlements in the Carolinas; Winsor, Narrative and Critical History of America, V, p. 304; Colonial Records of North Carolina, IV, p. xx; Weston, Documents Connected with the History of South Carolina, p. 82; Ellis and Evans, History of Lancaster County, Pa., chs. iii, xxvi.

‡ Parkman, Pontiac, II; Griffis, Sir William Johnson, p. 6; Simms's Frontiersmen of New York.

§ Monette, Mississippi Valley, I, p. 311.

‖ Wis. Hist. Cols., XI, p. 50; Hinsdale, Old Northwest, p. 121; Burke, "Oration on Conciliation," Works (1872 ed.), I, p. 473.

¶ Roosevelt, Winning of the West, and citations there given; Cutler's Life of Cutler.

and the Carolinas and eastern Georgia.* Beyond this region of continuous settlement were the small settled areas of Kentucky and Tennessee, and the Ohio, with the mountains intervening between them and the Atlantic area, thus giving a new and important character to the frontier. The isolation of the region increased its peculiarly American tendencies, and the need of transportation facilities to connect it with the East called out important schemes of internal improvement, which will be noted farther on. The "West," as a self-conscious section, began to evolve.

From decade to decade distinct advances of the frontier occurred. By the census of 1820 † the settled area included Ohio, southern Indiana and Illinois, southeastern Missouri, and about one-half of Louisiana. This settled area had surrounded Indian areas, and the management of these tribes became an object of political concern. The frontier region of the time lay along the Great Lakes, where Astor's American Fur Company operated in the Indian trade,‡ and beyond the Mississippi, where Indian traders extended their activity even to the Rocky Mountains; Florida also furnished frontier conditions. The Mississippi River region was the scene of typical frontier settlements.§

---

* Scribner's Statistical Atlas, xxxviii, pl. 13; MacMaster, Hist. of People of U. S., i, pp. 4, 60, 61; Imlay and Filson, Western Territory of America (London, 1793); Rochefoucault-Liancourt, Travels Through the United States of North America (London, 1799); Michaux's " Journal," in Proceedings American Philosophical Society, xxvi, No. 129; Forman, Narrative of a Journey Down the Ohio and Mississippi in 1780–'90 (Cincinnati, 1888); Bartram, Travels Through North Carolina, etc. (London, 1792); Pope, Tour Through the Southern and Western Territories, etc. (Richmond, 1792); Weld, Travels Through the States of North America (London, 1799); Baily, Journal of a Tour in the Unsettled States of North America, 1796–'97 (London, 1856); Pennsylvania Magazine of History, July, 1886; Winsor, Narrative and Critical History of America, vii, pp. 491, 492, citations.

† Scribner's Statistical Atlas, xxxix.

‡ Turner, Character and Influence of the Indian Trade in Wisconsin (Johns Hopkins University Studies, Series ix), pp. 61 ff.

§ Monette, History of the Mississippi Valley, ii; Flint, Travels and Residence in Mississippi; Flint, Geography and History of the Western States; Abridgment of Debates of Congress, vii, pp. 397, 398, 404; Holmes, Account of the U. S.; Kingdom, America and the British Colonies (London, 1820); Grund, Americans, ii, chs. i, iii, vi (although writing in 1836, he treats of conditions that grew out of western advance from the

The rising steam navigation* on western waters, the opening of the Erie Canal, and the westward extension of cotton† culture added five frontier states to the Union in this period. Grund, writing in 1836, declares: "It appears then that the universal disposition of Americans to emigrate to the western wilderness, in order to enlarge their dominion over inanimate nature, is the actual result of an expansive power which is inherent in them, and which by continually agitating all classes of society is constantly throwing a large portion of the whole population on the extreme confines of the State, in order to gain space for its development. Hardly is a new State or Territory formed before the same principle manifests itself again and gives rise to a further emigration; and so is it destined to go on until a physical barrier must finally obstruct its progress."‡

In the middle of this century the line indicated by the present eastern boundary of Indian Territory, Nebraska, and Kansas marked the frontier of the Indian country.§ Minnesota and

---

era of 1820 to that time); Peck, Guide for Emigrants (Boston, 1831); Darby, Emigrants' Guide to Western and Southwestern States and Territories; Dana, Geographical Sketches in the Western Country; Kinzie, Waubun; Keating, Narrative of Long's Expedition; Schoolcraft, Discovery of the Sources of the Mississippi River, Travels in the Central Portions of the Mississippi Valley, and Lead Mines of the Missouri; Andreas, History of Illinois, I, 86-99; Hurlbut, Chicago Antiquities; McKenney, Tour to the Lakes; Thomas, Travels through the Western Country, etc. (Auburn, N. Y., 1819).

* Darby, Emigrants' Guide, pp. 272 ff.; Benton, Abridgment of Debates, VII, p. 397.

† De Bow's Review, IV, p. 254; XVII, p. 428.

‡ Grund, Americans, II, p. 8.

§ Peck, New Guide to the West (Cincinnati, 1848), ch. IV; Parkman, Oregon Trail; Hall, The West (Cincinnati, 1848); Pierce, Incidents of Western Travel; Murray, Travels in North America; Lloyd, Steamboat Directory (Cincinnati, 1856); "Forty Days in a Western Hotel" (Chicago), in Putnam's Magazine, December, 1894; Mackay, The Western World, II, ch. II, III; Meeker, Life in the West; Bogen, German in America (Boston, 1851); Olmstead, Texas Journey; Greeley, Recollections of a Busy Life; Schouler, History of the United States, V, 261-267; Peyton, Over the Alleghanies and Across the Prairies (London, 1870); Loughborough, The Pacific Telegraph and Railway (St. Louis, 1849); Whitney, Project for a Railroad to the Pacific (New York, 1849); Peyton, Suggestions on Railroad Communication with the Pacific, and the Trade of China and the Indian Islands; Benton, Highway to the Pacific (a speech delivered in the U. S. Senate, December 16, 1850).

Wisconsin still exhibited frontier conditions,* but the distinctive frontier of the period is found in California, where the gold discoveries had sent a sudden tide of adventurous miners, and in Oregon, and the settlements in Utah.† As the frontier has leaped over the Alleghanies, so now it skipped the Great Plains and the Rocky Mountains; and in the same way that the advance of the frontiersmen beyond the Alleghanies had caused the rise of important questions of transportation and internal improvement, so now the settlers beyond the Rocky Mountains needed means of communication with the East, and in the furnishing of these arose the settlement of the Great Plains and the development of still another kind of frontier life. Railroads, fostered by land grants, sent an increasing tide of immigrants into the far West. The United States Army fought a series of Indian wars in Minnesota, Dakota, and the Indian Territory.

By 1880 the settled area had been pushed into northern Michigan, Wisconsin, and Minnesota, along Dakota rivers, and in the Black Hills region, and was ascending the rivers of Kansas and Nebraska. The development of mines in Colorado had drawn isolated frontier settlements into that region, and Montana and Idaho were receiving settlers. The frontier was found in these mining camps and the ranches of the Great Plains. The superintendent of the census for 1890 reports, as previously stated, that the settlements of the West lie so scattered over the region that there can no longer be said to be a frontier line.

In these successive frontiers we find natural boundary lines which have served to mark and to affect the characteristics of the frontiers, namely: The "fall line;" the Alleghany Mountains; the Mississippi; the Missouri, where its direction approximates north and south; the line of the arid lands, approximately the ninety-ninth meridian; and the Rocky Mountains. The fall line marked the frontier of the seventeenth century; the Alleghanies that of the eighteenth; the Mississippi that of

---

* A writer in The Home Missionary (1850), p. 239, reporting Wisconsin conditions, exclaims: "Think of this, people of the enlightened East. What an example, to come from the very frontiers of civilization!" But one of the missionaries writes: "In a few years Wisconsin will no longer be considered as the West, or as an outpost of civilization, any more than western New York, or the Western Reserve."

†Bancroft (H. H.), History of California, History of Oregon, and Popular Tribunals; Shinn, Mining Camps.

the first quarter of the nineteenth; the Missouri that of the middle of this century (omitting the California movement); and the belt of the Rocky Mountains and the arid tract, the present frontier. Each was won by a series of Indian wars.

THE FRONTIER FURNISHES A FIELD FOR COMPARATIVE STUDY OF SOCIAL DEVELOPMENT.

At the Atlantic frontier one can study the germs of processes repeated at each successive frontier. We have the complex European life sharply precipitated by the wilderness into the simplicity of primitive conditions. The first frontier had to meet its Indian question, its question of the disposition of the public domain, of the means of intercourse with older settlements, of the extension of political organization, of religious and educational activity. And the settlement of these and similar questions for one frontier served as a guide for the next. The American student needs not to go to the "prim little townships of Sleswick" for illustrations of the law of continuity and development. For example, he may study the origin of our land policies in the colonial land policy; he may see how the system grew by adapting the statutes to the customs of the successive frontiers.* He may see how the mining experience in the lead regions of Wisconsin, Illinois, and Iowa was applied to the mining laws of the Rockies,† and how our Indian policy has been a series of experimentations on successive frontiers. Each tier of new States has found in the older ones material for its constitutions.‡ Each frontier has made similar contributions to American character, as will be discussed farther on.

But with all these similarities there are essential differences, due to the place element and the time element. It is evident that the farming frontier of the Mississippi Valley presents different conditions from the mining frontier of the Rocky Mountains. The frontier reached by the Pacific Railroad, surveyed into rectangles, guarded by the United States Army, and recruited by the daily immigrant ship, moves forward at a swifter pace and in a different way than the frontier reached by the birch canoe or the pack horse. The geologist traces

---

* See the suggestive paper by Prof. Jesse Macy, The Institutional Beginnings of a Western State.

† Shinn, Mining Camps.

‡ Compare Thorpe, in Annals American Academy of Political and Social Science, September, 1891; Bryce, American Commonwealth (1888), II, p. 689.

patiently the shores of ancient seas, maps their areas, and compares the older and the newer. It would be a work worth the historian's labors to mark these various frontiers and in detail compare one with another. Not only would there result a more adequate conception of American development and characteristics, but invaluable additions would be made to the history of society.

Loria,* the Italian economist, has urged the study of colonial life as an aid in understanding the stages of European development, affirming that colonial settlement is for economic science what the mountain is for geology, bringing to light primitive stratifications. "America," he says, "has the key to the historical enigma which Europe has sought for centuries in vain, and the land which has no history reveals luminously the course of universal history." There is much truth in this. The United States lies like a huge page in the history of society. Line by line as we read this continental page from west to east we find the record of social evolution. It begins with the Indian and the hunter; it goes on to tell of the disintegration of savagery by the entrance of the trader, the pathfinder of civilization; we read the annals of the pastoral stage in ranch life; the exploitation of the soil by the raising of unrotated crops of corn and wheat in sparsely settled farming communities; the intensive culture of the denser farm settlement; and finally the manufacturing organization with city and factory system.† This page is familiar to the student of census statistics, but how little of it has been used by our historians. Particularly in eastern States this page is a palimpsest. What is now a manufacturing State was in an earlier decade an area of intensive farming. Earlier yet it had been a wheat area, and still earlier the "range" had attracted the cattle-herder. Thus Wisconsin, now developing manufacture, is a State with varied agricultural interests. But earlier it was given over to almost exclusive grain-raising, like North Dakota at the present time.

Each of these areas has had an influence in our economic

---

* Loria, Analisi della Proprieta Capitalista, II., p. 15.

† Compare Observations on the North American Land Company, London, 1796, pp. xv, 144; Logan, History of Upper South Carolina, I, pp. 149–151; Turner, Character and Influence of Indian Trade in Wisconsin, p. 18; Peck, New Guide for Emigrants (Boston, 1837), ch. iv; Compendium Eleventh Census, I, p. xl.

and political history; the evolution of each into a higher stage has worked political transformations. But what constitutional historian has made any adequate attempt to interpret political facts by the light of these social areas and changes?*

The Atlantic frontier was compounded of fisherman, fur-trader, miner, cattle-raiser, and farmer. Excepting the fisherman, each type of industry was on the march toward the West, impelled by an irresistible attraction. Each passed in successive waves across the continent. Stand at Cumberland Gap and watch the procession of civilization, marching single file— the buffalo following the trail to the salt springs, the Indian, the fur-trader and hunter, the cattle-raiser, the pioneer farmer— and the frontier has passed by. Stand at South Pass in the Rockies a century later and see the same procession with wider intervals between. The unequal rate of advance compels us to distinguish the frontier into the trader's frontier, the rancher's frontier, or the miner's frontier, and the farmer's frontier. When the mines and the cow pens were still near the fall line the traders' pack trains were tinkling across the Alleghanies, and the French on the Great Lakes were fortifying their posts, alarmed by the British trader's birch canoe. When the trappers scaled the Rockies, the farmer was still near the mouth of the Missouri.

THE INDIAN TRADER'S FRONTIER.

Why was it that the Indian trader passed so rapidly across the continent? What effects followed from the trader's frontier? The trade was coeval with American discovery. The Norsemen, Vespuccius, Verrazani, Hudson, John Smith, all trafficked for furs. The Plymouth pilgrims settled in Indian cornfields, and their first return cargo was of beaver and lumber. The records of the various New England colonies show how steadily exploration was carried into the wilderness by this trade. What is true for New England is, as would be expected, even plainer for the rest of the colonies. All along the coast from Maine to Georgia the Indian trade opened up the river courses. Steadily the trader passed westward, utilizing the older lines of French trade. The Ohio, the Great Lakes, the Mississippi, the Missouri, and the Platte, the lines of western advance, were ascended by traders. They found

---

* See pages 220, 221, 223, *post*, for illustrations of the political accompaniments of changed industrial conditions.

the passes in the Rocky Mountains and guided Lewis and Clarke,* Fremont, and Bidwell. The explanation of the rapidity of this advance is connected with the effects of the trader on the Indian. The trading post left the unarmed tribes at the mercy of those that had purchased fire-arms—a truth which the Iroquois Indians wrote in blood, and so the remote and unvisited tribes gave eager welcome to the trader. "The savages," wrote La Salle, "take better care of us French than of their own children; from us only can they get guns and goods." This accounts for the trader's power and the rapidity of his advance. Thus the disintegrating forces of civilization entered the wilderness. Every river valley and Indian trail became a fissure in Indian society, and so that society became honeycombed. Long before the pioneer farmer appeared on the scene, primitive Indian life had passed away. The farmers met Indians armed with guns. The trading frontier, while steadily undermining Indian power by making the tribes ultimately dependent on the whites, yet, through its sale of guns, gave to the Indians increased power of resistance to the farming frontier. French colonization was dominated by its trading frontier; English colonization by its farming frontier. There was an antagonism between the two frontiers as between the two nations. Said Duquesne to the Iroquois, "Are you ignorant of the difference between the king of England and the king of France? Go see the forts that our king has established and you will see that you can still hunt under their very walls. They have been placed for your advantage in places which you frequent. The English, on the contrary, are no sooner in possession of a place than the game is driven away. The forest falls before them as they advance, and the soil is laid bare so that you can scarce find the wherewithal to erect a shelter for the night."

And yet, in spite of this opposition of the interests of the trader and the farmer, the Indian trade pioneered the way for civilization. The buffalo trail became the Indian trail, and this because the trader's "trace;" the trails widened into roads, and the roads into turnpikes, and these in turn were transformed into railroads. The same origin can be shown for the railroads of the South, the far West, and the Dominion

---

* But Lewis and Clarke were the first to explore the route from the Missouri to the Columbia.

of Canada.* The trading posts reached by these trails were on the sites of Indian villages which had been placed in positions suggested by nature; and these trading posts, situated so as to command the water systems of the country, have grown into such cities as Albany, Pittsburg, Detroit, Chicago, St. Louis, Council Bluffs, and Kansas City. Thus civilization in America has followed the arteries made by geology, pouring an ever richer tide through them, until at last the slender paths of aboriginal intercourse have been broadened and interwoven into the complex mazes of modern commercial lines; the wilderness has been interpenetrated by lines of civilization growing ever more numerous. It is like the steady growth of a complex nervous system for the originally simple, inert continent. If one would understand why we are to-day one nation, rather than a collection of isolated states, he must study this economic and social consolidation of the country. In this progress from savage conditions lie topics for the evolutionist.†

The effect of the Indian frontier as a consolidating agent in our history is important. From the close of the seventeenth century various intercolonial congresses have been called to treat with Indians and establish common measures of defense. Particularism was strongest in colonies with no Indian frontier. This frontier stretched along the western border like a cord of union. The Indian was a common danger, demanding united action. Most celebrated of these conferences was the Albany congress of 1754, called to treat with the Six Nations, and to consider plans of union. Even a cursory reading of the plan proposed by the congress reveals the importance of the frontier. The powers of the general council and the officers were, chiefly, the determination of peace and war with the Indians, the regulation of Indian trade, the purchase of Indian lands, and the creation and government of new settlements as a security against the Indians. It is evident that the unifying tendencies of the Revolutionary period were facilitated by the previous cooperation in the regulation of the frontier. In this connection may be mentioned the importance of the frontier, from

---

* Narrative and Critical History of America, VIII, p. 10; Sparks' Washington Works, IX, pp. 303, 327; Logan, History of Upper South Carolina, I; McDonald, Life of Kenton, p. 72; Cong. Record, XXIII, p. 57.

† On the effect of the fur trade in opening the routes of migration, see the author's Character and Influence of the Indian Trade in Wisconsin.

that day to this, as a military training school, keeping alive the power of resistance to aggression, and developing the stalwart and rugged qualities of the frontiersman.

THE RANCHER'S FRONTIER.

It would not be possible in the limits of this paper to trace the other frontiers across the continent. Travelers of the eighteenth century found the "cowpens" among the canebrakes and peavine pastures of the South, and the "cow drivers" took their droves to Charleston, Philadelphia, and New York.* Travelers at the close of the War of 1812 met droves of more than a thousand cattle and swine from the interior of Ohio going to Pennsylvania to fatten for the Philadelphia market.† The ranges of the Great Plains, with ranch and cowboy and nomadic life, are things of yesterday and of to-day. The experience of the Carolina cowpens guided the ranchers of Texas. One element favoring the rapid extension of the rancher's frontier is the fact that in a remote country lacking transportation facilities the product must be in small bulk, or must be able to transport itself, and the cattle raiser could easily drive his product to market. The effect of these great ranches on the subsequent agrarian history of the localities in which they existed should be studied.

THE FARMER'S FRONTIER.

The maps of the census reports show an uneven advance of the farmer's frontier, with tongues of settlement pushed forward and with indentations of wilderness. In part this is due to Indian resistance, in part to the location of river valleys and passes, in part to the unequal force of the centers of frontier attraction. Among the important centers of attraction may be mentioned the following: fertile and favorably situated soils, salt springs, mines, and army posts.

ARMY POSTS.

The frontier army post, serving to protect the settlers from the Indians, has also acted as a wedge to open the Indian country, and has been a nucleus for settlement.‡ In this con-

---

* Lodge, English Colonies, p. 152 and citations; Logan, Hist. of Upper South Carolina, I, p. 151.

† Flint, Recollections, p. 9.

‡ See Monette, Mississippi Valley, I, p. 344.

nection mention should also be made of the Government military and exploring expeditions in determining the lines of settlement. But all the more important expeditions were greatly indebted to the earliest pathmakers, the Indian guides, the traders and trappers, and the French voyageurs, who were inevitable parts of governmental expeditions from the days of Lewis and Clarke.* Each expedition was an epitome of the previous factors in western advance.

SALT SPRINGS.

In an interesting monograph, Victor Hehn† has traced the effect of salt upon early European development, and has pointed out how it affected the lines of settlement and the form of administration. A similar study might be made for the salt springs of the United States. The early settlers were tied to the coast by the need of salt, without which they could not preserve their meats or live in comfort. Writing in 1752, Bishop Spangenburg says of a colony for which he was seeking lands in North Carolina, "They will require salt & other necessaries which they can neither manufacture nor raise. Either they must go to Charleston, which is 300 miles distant * * * Or else they must go to Boling's Point in Vᵃ on a branch of the James & is also 300 miles from here * * * Or else they must go down the Roanoke—I know not how many miles—where salt is brought up from the Cape Fear." ‡ This may serve as a typical illustration. An annual pilgrimage to the coast for salt thus became essential. Taking flocks or furs and ginseng root, the early settlers sent their pack trains after seeding time each year to the coast.§ This proved to be an important educational influence, since it was almost the only way in which the pioneer learned what was going on in the East. But when discovery was made of the salt springs of the Kanawha, and the Holston, and Kentucky, and central New York, the West began to be freed from dependence on the coast. It was in part the effect of finding these salt springs that enabled settlement to cross the mountains.

---

* Coues', Lewis and Clarke's Expedition, I, pp. 2, 253–259; Benton, in Cong. Record, XXIII, p. 57.

† Hehn, Das Salz (Berlin, 1873).

‡ Col. Records of N. C., V, p. 3.

§ Findley, History of the Insurrection in the Four Western Counties of Pennsylvania in the Year 1794 (Philadelphia, 1796), p. 35.

From the time the mountains rose between the pioneer and the seaboard, a new order of Americanism arose. The West and the East began to get out of touch of each other. The settlements from the sea to the mountains kept connection with the rear and had a certain solidarity. But the over-mountain men grew more and more independent. The East took a narrow view of American advance, and nearly lost these men. Kentucky and Tennessee history bears abundant witness to the truth of this statement. The East began to try to hedge and limit westward expansion. Though Webster could declare that there were no Alleghanies in his politics, yet in politics in general they were a very solid factor.

LAND.

The exploitation of the beasts took hunter and trader to the west, the exploitation of the grasses took the rancher west, and the exploitation of the virgin soil of the river valleys and prairies attracted the farmer. Good soils have been the most continuous attraction to the farmer's frontier. The land hunger of the Virginians drew them down the rivers into Carolina, in early colonial days; the search for soils took the Massachusetts men to Pennsylvania and to New York. As the eastern lands were taken up migration flowed across them to the west. Daniel Boone, the great backwoodsman, who combined the occupations of hunter, trader, cattle-raiser, farmer, and surveyor—learning, probably from the traders, of the fertility of the lands on the upper Yadkin, where the traders were wont to rest as they took their way to the Indians, left his Pennsylvania home with his father, and passed down the Great Valley road to that stream. Learning from a trader whose posts were on the Red River in Kentucky of its game and rich pastures, he pioneered the way for the farmers to that region. Thence he passed to the frontier of Missouri, where his settlement was long a landmark on the frontier. Here again he helped to open the way for civilization, finding salt licks, and trails, and land. His son was among the earliest trappers in the passes of the Rocky Mountains, and his party are said to have been the first to camp on the present site of Denver. His grandson, Col. A. J. Boone, of Colorado, was a power among the Indians of the Rocky Mountains, and was appointed an agent by the Government. Kit Carson's mother was a Boone.* Thus this family epitomizes the backwoods-man's advance across the continent.

The farmer's advance came in a distinct series of waves. In Peck's New Guide to the West, published in Boston in 1837, occurs this suggestive passage:

Generally, in all the western settlements, three classes, like the waves of the ocean, have rolled one after the other. First comes the pioneer, who depends for the subsistence of his family chiefly upon the natural growth of vegetation, called the "range," and the proceeds of hunting. His implements of agriculture are rude, chiefly of his own make, and his efforts directed mainly to a crop of corn and a "truck patch." The last is a rude garden for growing cabbage, beans, corn for roasting ears, cucumbers, and potatoes. A log cabin, and, occasionally, a stable and corn-crib, and a field of a dozen acres, the timber girdled or "deadened," and fenced, are enough for his occupancy. It is quite immaterial whether he ever becomes the owner of the soil. He is the occupant for the time being, pays no rent, and feels as independent as the "lord of the manor." With a horse, cow, and one or two breeders of swine, he strikes into the woods with his family, and becomes the founder of a new county, or perhaps state. He builds his cabin, gathers around him a few other families of similar tastes and habits, and occupies till the range is somewhat subdued, and hunting a little precarious, or, which is more frequently the case, till the neighbors crowd around, roads, bridges, and fields annoy him, and he lacks elbow room. The preemption law enables him to dispose of his cabin and cornfield to the next class of emigrants; and, to employ his own figures, he "breaks for the high timber," "clears out for the New Purchase," or migrates to Arkansas or Texas, to work the same process over.

The next class of emigrants purchase the lands, add field to field, clear out the roads, throw rough bridges over the streams, put up hewn log houses with glass windows and brick or stone chimneys, occasionally plant orchards, build mills, schoolhouses, court-houses, etc., and exhibit the picture and forms of plain, frugal, civilized life.

Another wave rolls on. The men of capital and enterprise come. The settler is ready to sell out and take the advantage of the rise in property, push farther into the interior and become, himself, a man of capital and enterprise in turn. The small village rises to a spacious town or city; substantial edifices of brick, extensive fields, orchards, gardens, colleges, and churches are seen. Broadcloths, silks, leghorns, crapes, and all the refinements, luxuries, elegancies, frivolities, and fashions are in vogue. Thus wave after wave is rolling westward; the real Eldorado is still farther on.

A portion of the two first classes remain stationary amidst the general movement, improve their habits and condition, and rise in the scale of society.

The writer has traveled much amongst the first class, the real pioneers. He has lived many years in connection with the second grade; and now

---

*Hale, Daniel Boone (pamphlet).

the third wave is sweeping over large districts of Indiana, Illinois, and Missouri. Migration has become almost a habit in the West. Hundreds of men can be found, not over 50 years of age, who have settled for the fourth, fifth, or sixth time on a new spot. To sell out and remove only a fe hundred miles makes up a portion of the variety of backwoods life and manners.*

Omitting those of the pioneer farmers who move from the love of adventure, the advance of the more steady farmer is easy to understand. Obviously the immigrant was attracted by the cheap lands of the frontier, and even the native farmer felt their influence strongly. Year by year the farmers who lived on soil whose returns were diminished by unrotated crops were offered the virgin soil of the frontier at nominal prices. Their growing families demanded more lands, and these were dear. The competition of the unexhausted, cheap, and easily tilled prairie lands compelled the farmer either to go west and continue the exhaustion of the soil on a new frontier, or to adopt intensive culture. Thus the census of 1890 shows, in the Northwest, many counties in which there is an absolute or a relative decrease of population. These States have been sending farmers to advance the frontier on the plains, and have themselves begun to turn to intensive farming and to manufacture. A decade before this, Ohio had shown the same transition stage. Thus the demand for land and the love of wilderness freedom drew the frontier ever onward.

Having now roughly outlined the various kinds of frontiers, and their modes of advance, chiefly from the point of view of the frontier itself, we may next inquire what were the influences on the East and on the Old World. A rapid enumeration of some of the more noteworthy effects is all that I have time for.

COMPOSITE NATIONALITY.

First, we note that the frontier promoted the formation of a composite nationality for the American people. The coast was preponderantly English, but the later tides of continental immigration flowed across to the free lands. This was the case from the early colonial days. The Scotch Irish and the Pala-

---

* Compare Baily, Tour in the Unsettled Parts of North America (London, 1856), pp. 217-219, where a similar analysis is made for 1796. See also Collot, Journey in North America (Paris, 1826), p. 109; Observations on the North American Land Company (London, 1796), pp. xv, 144; Logan, History of Upper South Carolina.

tine Germans, or "Pennsylvania Dutch," furnished the dominant element in the stock of the colonial frontier. With these peoples were also the freed indented servants, or redemptioners, who at the expiration of their time of service passed to the frontier. Governor Spottswood of Virginia writes in 1717, "The inhabitants of our frontiers are composed generally of such as have been transported hither as servants, and, being out of their time, settle themselves where land is to be taken up and that will produce the necessarys of life with little labour."* Very generally these redemptioners were of non-English stock. In the crucible of the frontier the immigrants were Americanized, liberated, and fused into a mixed race, English in neither nationality or characteristics. The process has gone on from the early days to our own. Burke and other writers in the middle of the eighteenth century believed that Pennsylvania† was "threatened with the danger of being wholly foreign in language, manners, and perhaps even inclinations." The German and Scotch-Irish elements in the frontier of the South were only less great. In the middle of the present century the German element in Wisconsin was already so considerable that leading publicists looked to the creation of a German state out of the commonwealth by concentrating their colonization.‡ Such examples teach us to beware of misinterpreting the fact that there is a common English speech in America into a belief that the stock is also English.

INDUSTRIAL INDEPENDENCE.

In another way the advance of the frontier decreased our dependence on England. The coast, particularly of the South, lacked diversified industries, and was dependent on England for the bulk of its supplies. In the South there was even a dependence on the Northern colonies for articles of food. Governor Glenn, of South Carolina, writes in the middle of the eighteenth century: "Our trade with New York and Philadelphia was of this sort, draining us of all the little money and bills we could gather from other places for their bread, flour, beer, hams, bacon, and other things of their produce, all which, except beer, our new townships begin to supply us with, which

---

* "Spottswood Papers," in Collections of Virginia Historical Society, I, II.

† [Burke], European Settlements, etc. (1765 ed.), II, p. 200.

‡ Everest, in Wisconsin Historical Collections, XII, pp. 7 ff

are settled with very industrious and thriving Germans. This no doubt diminishes the number of shipping and the appearance of our trade, but it is far from being a detriment to us."[*] Before long the frontier created a demand for merchants. As it retreated from the coast it became less and less possible for England to bring her supplies directly to the consumer's wharfs, and carry away staple crops, and staple crops began to give way to diversified agriculture for a time. The effect of this phase of the frontier action upon the northern section is perceived when we realize how the advance of the frontier aroused seaboard cities like Boston, New York, and Baltimore, to engage in rivalry for what Washington called "the extensive and valuable trade of a rising empire."

EFFECTS ON NATIONAL LEGISLATION.

The legislation which most developed the powers of the National Government, and played the largest part in its activity, was conditioned on the frontier. Writers have discussed the subjects of tariff, land, and internal improvement, as subsidiary to the slavery question. But when American history comes to be rightly viewed it will be seen that the slavery question is an incident. In the period from the end of the first half of the present century to the close of the civil war slavery rose to primary, but far from exclusive, importance. But this does not justify Dr. von Holst (to take an example) in treating our constitutional history in its formative period down to 1828 in a single volume, giving six volumes chiefly to the history of slavery from 1828 to 1861, under the title "Constitutional History of the United States." The growth of nationalism and the evolution of American political institutions were dependent on the advance of the frontier. Even so recent a writer as Rhodes, in his History of the United States since the compromise of 1850, has treated the legislation called out by the western advance as incidental to the slavery struggle.

This is a wrong perspective. The pioneer needed the goods of the coast, and so the grand series of internal improvement and railroad legislation began, with potent nationalizing effects. Over internal improvements occurred great debates, in which grave constitutional questions were discussed. Sectional groupings appear in the votes, profoundly significant for the

---

[*] Weston, Documents connected with History of South Carolina, p. 61.

historian.   Loose construction increased as the nation marched
westward.*   But the West was not content with bringing the
farm to the factory.   Under the lead of Clay—"Harry of the
West "—protective tariffs were passed, with the cry of bringing the factory to the farm.   The disposition of the public
lands was a third important subject of national legislation
influenced by the frontier.

THE PUBLIC DOMAIN.

The public domain has been a force of profound importance
in the nationalization and development of the Government.
The effects of the struggle of the landed and the landless States,
and of the ordinance of 1787, need no discussion. †   Adminis-
tratively the frontier called out some of the highest and most
vitalizing activities of the General Government.   The purchase
of Louisiana was perhaps the constitutional turning point in
the history of the Republic, inasmuch as it afforded both a new
area for national legislation and the occasion of the downfall
of the policy of strict construction.   But the purchase of Louisiana was called out by frontier needs and demands.   As frontier States accrued to the Union the national power grew.   In
a speech on the dedication of the Calhoun monument Mr.
Lamar explained: "In 1789 the States were the creators of the
Federal Government; in 1861 the Federal Government was
the creator of a large majority of the States."

When we consider the public domain from the point of view
of the sale and disposal of the public lands we are again brought
face to face with the frontier.   The policy of the United States
in dealing with its lands is in sharp contrast with the European
system of scientific administration.   Efforts to make this domain
a source of revenue, and to withhold it from emigrants in order
that settlement might be compact, were in vain.   The jealousy
and the fears of the East were powerless in the face of the
demands of the frontiersmen.   John Quincy Adams was obliged
to confess: "My own system of administration, which was to
make the national domain the inexhaustible fund for progress-
ive and unceasing internal improvement, has failed."   The

---

*See, for example, the speech of Clay, in the House of Representatives,
January 30, 1824.

†See the admirable monograph by Prof. H. B. Adams, Maryland's Influence on the Land Cessions; and also President Welling, in Papers\ American Historical Association, III, p. 411.

reason is obvious; a system of administration was not what the West demanded; it wanted land. Adams states the situation as follows: "The slaveholders of the South have bought the cooperation of the western country by the bribe of the western lands, abandoning to the new Western States their own proportion of the public property and aiding them in the design of grasping all the lands into their own hands. Thomas H. Benton was the author of this system, which he brought forward as a substitute for the American system of Mr. Clay, and to supplant him as the leading statesman of the West. Mr. Clay, by his tariff compromise with Mr. Calhoun, abandoned his own American system. At the same time he brought forward a plan for distributing among all the States of the Union the proceeds of the sales of the public lands. His bill for that purpose passed both Houses of Congress, but was vetoed by President Jackson, who, in his annual message of December, 1832, formally recommended that all public lands should be gratuitously given away to individual adventurers and to the States in which the lands are situated.*

"No subject," said Henry Clay, "which has presented itself to the present, or perhaps any preceding, Congress, is of greater magnitude than that of the public lands." When we consider the far-reaching effects of the Government's land policy upon political, economic, and social aspects of American life, we are disposed to agree with him. But this legislation was framed under frontier influences, and under the lead of Western statesmen like Benton and Jackson. Said Senator Scott of Indiana in 1841: "I consider the preemption law merely declaratory of the custom or common law of the settlers."

NATIONAL TENDENCIES OF THE FRONTIER.

It is safe to say that the legislation with regard to land, tariff, and internal improvements—the American system of the nationalizing Whig party—was conditioned on frontier ideas and needs. But it was not merely in legislative action that the frontier worked against the sectionalism of the coast. The economic and social characteristics of the frontier worked against sectionalism. The men of the frontier had closer resemblances to the Middle region than to either of the other sections. Pennsylvania had been the seed-plot of frontier emigration, and, although she passed on her settlers along the

---

*Adams Memoirs, IX, pp. 247, 248.

Great Valley into the west of Virginia and the Carolinas, yet the industrial society of these Southern frontiersmen was always more like that of the Middle region than like that of the tide-water portion of the South, which later came to spread its industrial type throughout the South.

The Middle region, entered by New York harbor, was an open door to all Europe. The tide-water part of the South represented typical Englishmen, modified by a warm climate and servile labor, and living in baronial fashion on great plantations; New England stood for a special English movement—Puritanism. The Middle region was less English than the other sections. It had a wide mixture of nationalities, a varied society, the mixed town and county system of local government, a varied economic life, many religious sects. In short, it was a region mediating between New England and the South, and the East and the West. It represented that composite nationality which the contemporary United States exhibits, that juxtaposition of non-English groups, occupying a valley or a little settlement, and presenting reflections of the map of Europe in their variety. It was democratic and nonsectional, if not national; "easy, tolerant, and contented;" rooted strongly in material prosperity. It was typical of the modern United States. It was least sectional, not only because it lay between North and South, but also because with no barriers to shut out its frontiers from its settled region, and with a system of connecting waterways, the Middle region mediated between East and West as well as between North and South. Thus it became the typically American region. Even the New Englander, who was shut out from the frontier by the Middle region, tarrying in New York or Pennsylvania on his westward march, lost the acuteness of his sectionalism on the way.*

The spread of cotton culture into the interior of the South finally broke down the contrast between the "tide-water" region and the rest of the State, and based Southern interests on slavery. Before this process revealed its results the western portion of the South, which was akin to Pennsylvania in stock, society, and industry, showed tendencies to fall away from the faith of the fathers into internal improvement legislation and nationalism. In the Virginia convention of 1829-'30, called to revise the constitution, Mr. Leigh, of Chesterfield, one of the tide-water counties, declared:

---

*Author's article in The Ægis (Madison, Wis.), November 4, 1892.

One of the main causes of discontent which led to this convention, that which had the strongest influence in overcoming our veneration for the work of our fathers, which taught us to contemn the sentiments of Henry and Mason and Pendleton, which weaned us from our reverence for the constituted authorities of the State, was an overweening passion for internal improvement. I say this with perfect knowledge, for it has been avowed to me by gentlemen from the West over and over again. And let me tell the gentleman from Albemarle (Mr. Gordon) that it has been another principal object of those who set this ball of revolution in motion, to overturn the doctrine of State rights, of which Virginia has been the very pillar, and to remove the barrier she has interposed to the interference of the Federal Government in that same work of internal improvement, by so reorganizing the legislature that Virginia, too, may be hitched to the Federal car.

It was this nationalizing tendency of the West that transformed the democracy of Jefferson into the national republicanism of Monroe and the democracy of Andrew Jackson. The West of the war of 1812, the West of Clay, and Benton, and Harrison, and Andrew Jackson, shut off by the Middle States and the mountains from the coast sections, had a solidarity of its own with national tendencies.[*] On the tide of the Father of Waters, North and South met and mingled into a nation. Interstate migration went steadily on—a process of cross-fertilization of ideas and institutions. The fierce struggle of the sections over slavery on the western frontier does not diminish the truth of this statement; it proves the truth of it. Slavery was a sectional trait that would not down, but in the West it could not remain sectional. It was the greatest of frontiersmen who declared: "I believe this Government can not endure permanently half slave and half free. It will become all of one thing or all of the other." Nothing works for nationalism like intercourse within the nation. Mobility of population is death to localism, and the western frontier worked irresistibly in unsettling population. The effects reached back from the frontier and affected profoundly the Atlantic coast and even the Old World.

GROWTH OF DEMOCRACY.

But the most important effect of the frontier has been in the promotion of democracy here and in Europe. As has been indicated, the frontier is productive of individualism. Complex society is precipitated by the wilderness into a kind of

---

[*] Compare Roosevelt, Thomas Benton, ch. i.

primitive organization based on the family. The tendency is anti-social. It produces antipathy to control, and particularly to any direct control. The tax-gatherer is viewed as a representative of oppression. Prof. Osgood, in an able article,[*] has pointed out that the frontier conditions prevalent in the colonies are important factors in the explanation of the American Revolution, where individual liberty was sometimes confused with absence of all effective government. The same conditions aid in explaining the difficulty of instituting a strong government in the period of the confederacy. The frontier individualism has from the beginning promoted democracy.

The frontier States that came into the Union in the first quarter of a century of its existence came in with democratic suffrage provisions, and had reactive effects of the highest importance upon the older States whose peoples were being attracted there. An extension of the franchise became essential. It was *western* New York that forced an extension of suffrage in the constitutional convention of that State in 1821; and it was *western* Virginia that compelled the tide-water region to put a more liberal suffrage provision in the constitution framed in 1830, and to give to the frontier region a more nearly proportionate representation with the tide-water aristocracy. The rise of democracy as an effective force in the nation came in with western preponderance under Jackson and William Henry Harrison, and it meant the triumph of the frontier—with all of its good and with all of its evil elements.[†] An interesting illustration of the tone of frontier democracy in 1830 comes from the same debates in the Virginia convention already referred to. A representative from western Virginia declared:

But, sir, it is not the increase of population in the West which this gentleman ought to fear. It is the energy which the mountain breeze and western habits impart to those emigrants. They are regenerated, politically I mean, sir. They soon become *working politicians;* and the difference, sir, between a *talking* and a *working* politican is immense. The Old Dominion has long been celebrated for producing great orators; the ablest metaphysicians in policy; men that can split hairs in all abstruse questions of political economy. But at home, or when they return from Congress, they have negroes to fan them asleep. But a Pennsylvania, a New York, an Ohio, or a western Virginia statesman, though far inferior in logic, metaphysics, and rhetoric to an old Virginia statesman, has this advantage, that when he returns home he takes off his coat and takes hold

---

[*] Political Science Quarterly, II, p. 457. Compare Sumner, Alexander Hamilton, Chs. ii–vii.

[†] Compare Wilson, Division and Reunion, pp. 15, 24.

of the plow. This gives him bone and muscle, sir, and preserves his republican principles pure and uncontaminated.

So long as free land exists, the opportunity for a competency exists, and economic power secures political power. But the democracy born of free land, strong in selfishness and individualism, intolerant of administrative experience and education, and pressing individual liberty beyond its proper bounds, has its dangers as well as it benefits. Individualism in America has allowed a laxity in regard to governmental affairs which has rendered possible the spoils system and all the manifest evils that follow from the lack of a highly developed civic spirit. In this connection may be noted also the influence of frontier conditions in permitting lax business honor, inflated paper currency and wild-cat banking. The colonial and revolutionary frontier was the region whence emanated many of the worst forms of an evil currency.* The West in the war of 1812 repeated the phenomenon on the frontier of that day, while the speculation and wild-cat banking of the period of the crisis of 1837 occurred on the new frontier belt of the next tier of States. Thus each one of the periods of lax financial integrity coincides with periods when a new set of frontier communities had arisen, and coincides in area with these successive frontiers, for the most part. The recent Populist agitation is a case in point. Many a State that now declines any connection with the tenets of the Populists, itself adhered to such ideas in an earlier stage of the development of the State. A primitive society can hardly be expected to show the intelligent appreciation of the complexity of business interests in a developed society. The continual recurrence of these areas of paper-money agitation is another evidence that the frontier can be isolated and studied as a factor in American history of the highest importance.†

---

* On the relation of frontier conditions to Revolutionary taxation, see Sumner, Alexander Hamilton, Ch. iii.

† I have refrained from dwelling on the lawless characteristics of the frontier, because they are sufficiently well known. The gambler and desperado, the regulators of the Carolinas and the vigilantes of California, are types of that line of scum that the waves of advancing civilization bore before them, and of the growth of spontaneous organs of authority where legal authority was absent. Compare Barrows, United States of Yesterday and To-morrow; Shinn, Mining Camps; and Bancroft, Popular Tribunals. The humor, bravery, and rude strength, as well as the vices of the frontier in its worst aspect, have left traces on American character, language, and literature, not soon to be effaced.

ATTEMPTS TO CHECK AND REGULATE THE FRONTIER.

The East has always feared the result of an unregulated
advance of the frontier, and has tried to check and guide it.
The English authorities would have checked settlement at
the headwaters of the Atlantic tributaries and allowed the
"savages to enjoy their deserts in quiet lest the peltry trade
should decrease." This called out Burke's splendid protest:

> If you stopped your grants, what would be the consequence? The
> people would occupy without grants. They have already so occupied in
> many places. You can not station garrisons in every part of these deserts.
> If you drive the people from one place, they will carry on their annual
> tillage and remove with their flocks and herds to another. Many of the
> people in the back settlements are already little attached to particular
> situations. Already they have topped the Appalachian mountains. From
> thence they behold before them an immense plain, one vast, rich, level
> meadow; a square of five hundred miles. Over this they would wander
> without a possibility of restraint; they would change their manners with
> their habits of life; would soon forget a government by which they were
> disowned; would become hordes of English Tartars; and, pouring down
> upon your unfortified frontiers a fierce and irresistible cavalry, become
> masters of your governors and your counselors, your collectors and comp-
> trollers, and of all the slaves that adhered to them. Such would, and in
> no long time must, be the effect of attempting to forbid as a crime and to
> suppress as an evil the command and blessing of Providence, "Increase
> and multiply." Such would be the happy result of an endeavor to keep
> as a lair of wild beasts that earth which God, by an express charter, has
> given to the children of men.

But the English Government was not alone in its desire to
limit the advance of the frontier and guide its destinies. Tide-
water Virginia * and South Carolina † gerrymandered those
colonies to insure the dominance of the coast in their legis-
latures. Washington desired to settle a State at a time in the
Northwest; Jefferson would reserve from settlement the territory of his Louisiana purchase north of the thirty-second par-
allel, in order to offer it to the Indians in exchange for their
settlements east of the Mississippi. "When we shall be full
on this side," he writes, "we may lay off a range of States on
the western bank from the head to the mouth, and so range
after range, advancing compactly as we multiply." Madison
went so far as to argue to the French minister that the United
States had no interest in seeing population extend itself on

---

* Debates in the Constitutional Convention, 1829–1830.
† [McCrady] Eminent and Representative Men of the Carolinas, I, p.43;
Calhoun's Works. I, pp. 401–406.

the right bank of the Mississippi, but should rather fear it. When the Oregon question was under debate, in 1824, Smyth, of Virginia, would draw an unchangeable line for the limits of the United States at the outer limit of two tiers of States beyond the Mississippi, complaining that the seaboard States were being drained of the flower of their population by the bringing of too much land into market. Even Thomas Benton, the man of widest views of the destiny of the West, at this stage of his career declared that along the ridge of the Rocky mountains "the western limits of the Republic should be drawn, and the statue of the fabled god Terminus should be raised upon its highest peak, never to be thrown down."* But the attempts to limit the boundaries, to restrict land sales and settlement, and to deprive the West of its share of political power were all in vain. Steadily the frontier of settlement advanced and carried with it individualism, democracy, and nationalism, and powerfully affected the East and the Old World.

MISSIONARY ACTIVITY.

The most effective efforts of the East to regulate the frontier came through its educational and religious activity, exerted by interstate migration and by organized societies. Speaking in 1835, Dr. Lyman Beecher declared: "It is equally plain that the religious and political destiny of our nation is to be decided in the West," and he pointed out that the population of the West "is assembled from all the States of the Union and from all the nations of Europe, and is rushing in like the waters of the flood, demanding for its moral preservation the immediate and universal action of those institutions which discipline the mind and arm the conscience and the heart. And so various are the opinions and habits, and so recent and imperfect is the acquaintance, and so sparse are the settlements of the West, that no homogeneous public sentiment can be formed to legislate immediately into being the requisite institutions. And yet they are all needed immediately in their utmost perfection and power. A nation is being 'born in a day.' * * * But what will become of the West if her prosperity rushes up to such a majesty of power, while those great institutions linger which are necessary to form the mind and the conscience and the heart of that vast world. It must not

---

* Speech in the Senate, March 1, 1825; Register of Debates, I, 721.

be permitted. * * * Let no man at the East quiet himself
and dream of liberty, whatever may become of the West.
* * * Her destiny is our destiny." *

With the appeal to the conscience of New England, he adds
appeals to her fears lest other religious sects anticipate her
own. The New England preacher and school-teacher left their
mark on the West. The dread of Western emancipation from
New England's political and economic control was paralled by
her fears lest the West cut loose from her religion. Com-
menting in 1850 on reports that settlement was rapidly
extending northward in Wisconsin, the editor of the Home
Missionary writes: "We scarcely know whether to rejoice or
mourn over this extension of our settlements. While we sym-
pathize in whatever tends to increase the physical resources
and prosperity of our country, we can not forget that with all
these dispersions into remote and still remoter corners of the
land the supply of the means of grace is becoming relatively
less and less." Acting in accordance with such ideas, home
missions were established and Western colleges were erected.
As seaboard cities like Philadelphia, New York, and Baltimore
strove for the mastery of Western trade, so the various denomi-
nations strove for the possession of the West. Thus an
intellectual stream from New England sources fertilized the
West. Other sections sent their missionaries; but the real
struggle was between sects. The contest for power and the
expansive tendency furnished to the various sects by the existence of a moving frontier must have had important results
on the character of religious organization in the United States.
The multiplication of rival churches in the little frontier
towns had deep and lasting social effects. The religious
aspects of the frontier make a chapter in our history which
needs study.

INTELLECTUAL TRAITS.

From the conditions of frontier life came intellectual traits
of profound importance. The works of travelers along each
frontier from colonial days onward describe certain common
traits, and these traits have, while softening down, still per-
sisted as survivals in the place of their origin, even when a
higher social organization succeeded. The result is that to the
frontier the American intellect owes its striking characteristics.
That coarseness and strength combined with acuteness and

---

*Plea for the West (Cincinnati, 1835), pp. 11 ff.

inquisitiveness; that practical, inventive turn of mind, quick to find expedients; that masterful grasp of material things, lacking in the artistic but powerful to effect great ends; that restless, nervous energy;* that dominant individualism, working for good and for evil, and withal that buoyancy and exuberance which comes with freedom—these are traits of the frontier, or traits called out elsewhere because of the existence of the frontier. Since the days when the fleet of Columbus sailed into the waters of the New World, America has been another name for opportunity, and the people of the United States have taken their tone from the incessant expansion which has not only been open but has even been forced upon them. He would be a rash prophet who should assert that the expansive character of American life has now entirely ceased. Movement has been its dominant fact, and, unless this training has no effect upon a people, the American energy will continually demand a wider field for its exercise. But never again will such gifts of free land offer themselves. For a moment, at the frontier, the bonds of custom are broken and unrestraint is triumphant. There is not *tabula rasa*. The stubborn American environment is there with its imperious summons to accept its conditions; the inherited ways of doing things are also there; and yet, in spite of environment, and in spite of custom, each frontier did indeed furnish a new field of opportunity, a gate of escape from the bondage of the past; and freshness, and confidence, and scorn of older society, impatience of its restraints and its ideas, and indifference to its lessons, have accompanied the frontier. What the Mediterranean Sea was to the Greeks, breaking the bond of custom, offering new experiences, calling out new institutions and activities, that, and more, the ever retreating frontier has been to the United States directly, and to the nations of Europe more remotely. And now, four centuries from the discovery of America, at the end of a hundred years of life under the Constitution, the frontier has gone, and with its going has closed the first period of American history.

---

* Colonial travelers agree in remarking on the phlegmatic characteristics of the colonists. It has frequently been asked how such a people could have developed that strained nervous energy now characteristic of them. Compare Sumner, Alexander Hamilton, p. 98, and Adams's History of the United States, I, p. 60; IX, pp. 240, 241. The transition appears to become marked at the close of the war of 1812, a period when interest centered upon the development of the West, and the West was noted for restless energy. Grund, Americans, II., ch. i.